A Tower too Tall

Original edition published in Japan by
Shiko Sha Company, Ltd., Tokyo, Japan, 1976
© 1976 Shiko Sha Company Ltd., illustrations
© 1979 Judson Press, English text adapted by Mildred Schell.

Published in the U.S.A. in 1979 by Judson Press, Valley Forge, PA 19481

Printed in Japan

ISBN 0-8170-0823-3

The name JUDSON PRESS is registered as a trademark in the U.S. Patent
Office.

A Tower Too Tall

Retold by Mildred Schell
from a story by Masahiro Kasuya

Judson Press ® Valley Forge

3680

Did you and your friend ever try to make a tower out of stones?

If you were careful and put each stone in the right place—just so—
the tower grew and grew, until
it was almost as tall as you are.

But, if even one stone was put in the wrong place,
whoosh!
                the whole tower
                                    came
                                            tumbling
                                                    down!

One day, a long time ago, in a land far away,
the king was out riding his horse.
He watched as some children put the last stone
on top of a tower they were making.

The children waited to see if their tower
would stand
                    or
                         come
                              tumbling
                                   down.
The tower stood tall.
The children laughed and waved their arms.
They were having fun.
They were glad they had made a good tower.

When the king got home, he climbed to the top of his palace.
He looked up at the sky.
He kept thinking about the children and their tower of stone.
Then, the king had an idea.
He sent for his people.

When the people came, the king said:
"My people, we have a beautiful city.
Now we need something else.
Let us build a big tower—so tall
that it will reach all the way to the heavens.
Then we shall be the most important people in the whole world."

The people cheered.
They said, "Yes, we shall build the tall tower."

Day after day, the people worked together on the tower.
They worked from early in the morning
until the sun went down at night.
They never got cross with each other.
They wanted to finish the tall tower.
They thought it would make them
more important than all the other people in the world.

They worked together.
They said:
"When the tower is finished,
we will be the best people
in the whole world.
Our king will be the
most important king.
He will be even more
important than God."

Day after day, the tower grew taller and taller.
One day it reached above the clouds.
No one could even see its top!
The king smiled.
"Now, we are better than anyone else,
for we have the tall tower," he said.

The people answered,
"O king, you are the greatest king of all.
Everyone will have to do what you say.
Our tall tower makes us
better than anyone else!
Nothing can stop us now!"

But they were wrong.

SUDDENLY
      the sky got dark;
      the wind blew very hard;
      there was loud thunder
        and bright lightning;
      the ground shook under their feet.
Everyone was afraid.

                When the earthquake was over,
                the people looked for their tower.
                It was gone!
                Where the tall tower had been,
                there was only a pile of rocks and stones.

Everyone began to talk at once, but—
it was just a babel of noise, for
they no longer spoke the same language.

Even best friends
found it hard to
understand one another.

The people no longer wanted to work together.
When the king spoke to them, they did not listen.
They began to leave their city.
Soon everyone was gone.

Only the broken tower was left
in the once beautiful city of Babel.

When you and your best friend build a tower of stones,
you are not trying to be important;
you are just having fun.

If your tower
            comes
                    tumbling down,

                    you can laugh and begin all over again,
                    because it is fun to be friends and
                    build towers together.